NovelReady

This planner belongs to:

_____

_____

_____

For more on story structure, plot, and character development, check out our website:

www.novelready.com

©2018 NovelReady, LLC. All rights reserved.

About This Planner

There are many ways to write a novel. The NovelReady Planner uses a generic three-act structure, applicable to many genres, but generally assumes you are writing a story with an active main character.

It is designed to start with character and build from there but is flexible enough for you to work in any order - or no order. Feel free to skip around!

How This Planner Is Organized

Basics > **Characters** > Major > Minor > **Plots** > Timelines > Subplots > **Acts** > **Scenes**

- Story Basics

    Answer some basic questions and jot down highlights of the backstory.

- Develop the Major Characters

    Get to know your Protagonist, Antagonist and other major characters. Craft personalities that will mirror and conflict. Explore how characters might change over the course of the story.

- Develop the Minor Characters

    Avoid flat characters by giving your minor characters goals and fears.

- Build Integrated Plot LInes

    Come up with the broad strokes of your major story lines. Complete mind maps to tie your setting, theme, plots and sub plots together.

- Outline Acts

    Worksheets for all three acts help you hit required plot milestones, show how your characters are changing, and generate scene ideas.

- Outline Scenes

    Individual Scene Sheets for up to 60 scenes. Work in chronological order or do milestone scenes first and then fill in the gaps. Ensure each scene affects your reader, your Protagonist, and contributes to your story.

Pro-Tip: Start in PENCIL.

Basics > Characters > Major > Minor > Plots > Timelines > Subplots > Acts > Scenes

Story Basics

Premise:

Genre:

Possible Titles:

Central Problem:

Why can't Ⓟ solve **Central Problem** immediately?

Theme:

Inspiration/Sources:

Ⓟ = Protagonist   Ⓐ = Antagonist

Basics > Characters > Major > Minor > Plots > Timelines > Subplots > Acts > Scenes

Backstory

Basics > **Characters** > Major > Minor > Plots > Timelines > Subplots > Acts > Scenes

Character Map

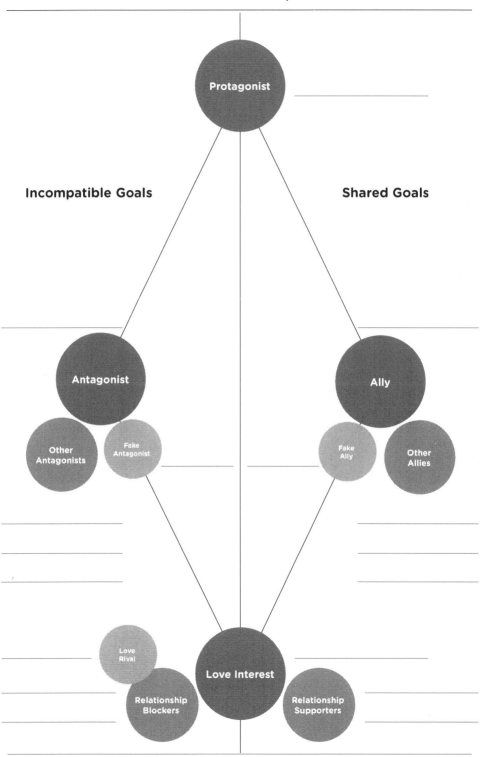

Basics > **Characters** > Major > Minor > Plots > Timelines > Subplots > Acts > Scenes

Character List

Character	Story Goal	Relationship to ⓟ

Basics > **Characters** > **Major** > Minor > Plots > Timelines > Subplots > Acts > Scenes

Who Is Your Protagonist?

◀╌╌▶
Introvert   Ambivert   Extrovert

◀╌╌▶
Self-Conscious   Relaxed   Charismatic

◀╌╌▶
Serious   Calm   Intense

◀╌╌▶
Methodical   Predictable   Innovative

◀╌╌▶
Thoughtful   Stable   Bias for Action

◀╌╌▶
Cautious   Reliable   Reckless

◀╌╌▶
Unassuming   Confident   Dominant

◀╌╌▶
Avoids Conflict   Seeks Harmony   Embraces Conflict

◀╌╌▶
Skeptical   Factual   Trusting

◀╌╌▶
Pessimistic   Optimistic   Enthusiastic

◀╌╌▶
Dutiful   Respectful   Rebellious

◀╌╌▶
Quiet   Communicative   Uninhibited

◀╌╌▶
Rigid   Flexible   Spontaneous

◀╌╌▶
Possessive   Permissive   Obsessive

◀╌╌▶
Formal   Casual   Disorganized

◀╌╌▶
Fastidious   Neat   Disheveled

◀╌╌▶
Analytical   Understanding   Emotional

◀╌╌▶
Jaded   Unpretentious   Naive

◀╌╌▶
Eager   Acquisitive   Rapacious

◀╌╌▶
Self-sacrificing   Caring   Selfish

TIP: Map where your ⓟ begins, then use arrows or color to show how ⓟ changes.

Basics > **Characters** > **Major** > Minor > Plots > Timelines > Subplots > Acts > Scenes

Character Sketch: Protagonist

Name	Appearance
Age / Occupation	
Psyche ❏ Ready for Change ❏ Resistant to Change	
Values	Key Traits
Fears	

Will character become a new person? In what way?

Snapshot (Before)	**Snapshot** (After)

Basics > **Characters** > **Major** > Minor > Plots > Timelines > Subplots > Acts > Scenes

Character Arc: Protagonist

Firmly Held (Mis)Belief

Effect (If the belief is true, how is the character being hurt in the beginning by clinging to it? If false, how is character hurting others by clinging to the belief instead of the truth?)

Cause (What life experiences support character's (mis)belief?)

Will character relinquish the (mis)belief?

Story Goal(s)

Basics > **Characters** > **Major** > Minor > Plots > Timelines > Subplots > Acts > Scenes

Character Bio: Protagonist

Who is this character just before the story starts? How did they get to this point?

Basics > **Characters** > **Major** > Minor > Plots > Timelines > Subplots > Acts > Scenes

Who Is Your Antagonist?

Introvert	Ambivert	Extrovert
Self-Conscious	Relaxed	Charismatic
Serious	Calm	Intense
Methodical	Predictable	Innovative
Thoughtful	Stable	Bias for Action
Cautious	Reliable	Reckless
Unassuming	Confident	Dominant
Avoids Conflict	Seeks Harmony	Embraces Conflict
Skeptical	Factual	Trusting
Pessimistic	Optimistic	Enthusiastic
Dutiful	Respectful	Rebellious
Quiet	Communicative	Uninhibited
Rigid	Flexible	Spontaneous
Possessive	Permissive	Obsessive
Formal	Casual	Disorganized
Fastidious	Neat	Disheveled
Analytical	Understanding	Emotional
Jaded	Unpretentious	Naive
Eager	Acquisitive	Rapacious
Self-sacrificing	Caring	Selfish

Basics > **Characters** > **Major** > Minor > Plots > Timelines > Subplots > Acts > Scenes

Character Sketch: Antagonist

Name	Appearance
Age / Occupation	
Psyche ❏ Ready for Change ❏ Resistant to Change	
Values	Key Traits
Fears	

Will character become a new person? In what way?

Snapshot (Before) | **Snapshot** (After)

Basics > **Characters** > **Major** > Minor > Plots > Timelines > Subplots > Acts > Scenes

Character Arc: Antagonist

Firmly Held (Mis)Belief

Effect (If the belief is true, how is the character being hurt in the beginning by clinging to it? If false, how is character hurting others by clinging to the belief instead of the truth?)

Cause (What life experiences support character's (mis)belief?)

Will character relinquish the (mis)belief?

Story Goal(s)

Basics > **Characters** > **Major** > Minor > Plots > Timelines > Subplots > Acts > Scenes

Character Bio: Antagonist

Who is this character just before the story starts? How did they get to this point?

Basics > **Characters** > **Major** > Minor > Plots > Timelines > Subplots > Acts > Scenes

Who Is Your Love Interest?

Introvert	Ambivert	Extrovert
Self-Conscious	Relaxed	Charismatic
Serious	Calm	Intense
Methodical	Predictable	Innovative
Thoughtful	Stable	Bias for Action
Cautious	Reliable	Reckless
Unassuming	Confident	Dominant
Avoids Conflict	Seeks Harmony	Embraces Conflict
Skeptical	Factual	Trusting
Pessimistic	Optimistic	Enthusiastic
Dutiful	Respectful	Rebellious
Quiet	Communicative	Uninhibited
Rigid	Flexible	Spontaneous
Possessive	Permissive	Obsessive
Formal	Casual	Disorganized
Fastidious	Neat	Disheveled
Analytical	Understanding	Emotional
Jaded	Unpretentious	Naive
Eager	Acquisitive	Rapacious
Self-sacrificing	Caring	Selfish

Basics > **Characters** > **Major** > Minor > Plots > Timelines > Subplots > Acts > Scenes

Character Sketch: Love Interest

Name	Appearance
Age	Occupation	

Psyche
❏ Ready for Change   ❏ Resistant to Change

Values	Key Traits

Fears

Will character become a new person? In what way?

Snapshot (Before)

Snapshot (After)

Basics > **Characters** > **Major** > Minor > Plots > Timelines > Subplots > Acts > Scenes

Character Arc: Love Interest

Firmly Held (Mis)Belief

Effect (If the belief is true, how is the character being hurt in the beginning by clinging to it? If false, how is character hurting others by clinging to the belief instead of the truth?)

Cause (What life experiences support character's (mis)belief?)

Will character relinquish the (mis)belief?

Story Goal(s)

Basics > **Characters** > **Major** > Minor > Plots > Timelines > Subplots > Acts > Scenes

Character Bio: Love Interest

Who is this character just before the story starts? How did they get to this point?

Basics > **Characters** > **Major** > Minor > Plots > Timelines > Subplots > Acts > Scenes

Who Is Your Ally?

Introvert	Ambivert	Extrovert
Self-Conscious	Relaxed	Charismatic
Serious	Calm	Intense
Methodical	Predictable	Innovative
Thoughtful	Stable	Bias for Action
Cautious	Reliable	Reckless
Unassuming	Confident	Dominant
Avoids Conflict	Seeks Harmony	Embraces Conflict
Skeptical	Factual	Trusting
Pessimistic	Optimistic	Enthusiastic
Dutiful	Respectful	Rebellious
Quiet	Communicative	Uninhibited
Rigid	Flexible	Spontaneous
Possessive	Permissive	Obsessive
Formal	Casual	Disorganized
Fastidious	Neat	Disheveled
Analytical	Understanding	Emotional
Jaded	Unpretentious	Naive
Eager	Acquisitive	Rapacious
Self-sacrificing	Caring	Selfish

Basics > **Characters** > **Major** > Minor > Plots > Timelines > Subplots > Acts > Scenes

Character Sketch: Ally

Name	Appearance
Age / Occupation	
Psyche ❏ Ready for Change ❏ Resistant to Change	
Values	Key Traits
Fears	

Will character become a new person? In what way?

Snapshot (Before)	**Snapshot** (After)

Basics > **Characters** > **Major** > Minor > Plots > Timelines > Subplots > Acts > Scenes

Character Arc: Ally

Firmly Held (Mis)Belief

Effect (If the belief is true, how is the character being hurt in the beginning by clinging to it? If false, how is character hurting others by clinging to the belief instead of the truth?)

Cause (What life experiences support character's (mis)belief?)

Will character relinquish the (mis)belief?

Story Goal(s)

Basics > **Characters** > **Major** > Minor > Plots > Timelines > Subplots > Acts > Scenes

Character Bio: Ally

Who is this character just before the story starts? How did they get to this point?

Basics > **Characters** > Major > **Minor** > Plots > Timelines > Subplots > Acts > Scenes

Minor Characters

Name	Age	Appearance
Role		
Relationship to ⓟ		
Values		Traits
Fears		

Snapshot: Who is this character before the story starts? (goals, worries, etc.)

Story Goal(s)

Name	Age	Appearance
Role		
Relationship to ⓟ		
Values		Traits
Fears		

Snapshot: (Who is this caracter before the story starts? [goals, worries, etc.])

Story Goal(s)

ⓟ = Protagonist   ⓐ = Antagonist

Basics > **Characters** > Major > **Minor** > Plots > Timelines > Subplots > Acts > Scenes

Minor Characters

Name	Age	Appearance
Role		
Relationship to ⓟ		
Values		Traits
Fears		

Snapshot: Who is this character before the story starts? (goals, worries, etc.)

Story Goal(s)

Name	Age	Appearance
Role		
Relationship to ⓟ		
Values		Traits
Fears		

Snapshot: (Who is this caracter before the story starts? [goals, worries, etc.])

Story Goal(s)

ⓟ = Protagonist   ⓐ = Antagonist

Basics > **Characters** > Major > **Minor** > Plots > Timelines > Subplots > Acts > Scenes

Minor Characters

Name	Age	Appearance
Role		
Relationship to Ⓟ		
Values		Traits
Fears		

Snapshot: Who is this character before the story starts? (goals, worries, etc.)

Story Goal(s)

Name	Age	Appearance
Role		
Relationship to Ⓟ		
Values		Traits
Fears		

Snapshot: (Who is this caracter before the story starts? [goals, worries, etc.])

Story Goal(s)

Ⓟ = Protagonist   Ⓐ = Antagonist

Basics > **Characters** > Major > **Minor** > Plots > Timelines > Subplots > Acts > Scenes

Minor Characters

Name	Age	Appearance
Role		
Relationship to Ⓟ		
Values		Traits
Fears		

Snapshot: Who is this character before the story starts? (goals, worries, etc.)

Story Goal(s)

Name	Age	Appearance
Role		
Relationship to Ⓟ		
Values		Traits
Fears		

Snapshot: (Who is this caracter before the story starts? [goals, worries, etc.])

Story Goal(s)

Ⓟ = Protagonist   Ⓐ = Antagonist

Plot Lines

Basics > Characters > Major > Minor > **Plots** > Timelines > Subplots > Acts > Scenes

Getting to Plot

In this section, you'll think about the arcs of your story's major ***plot lines***. These plot lines won't get equal weight, but they will share a similar structure, from an inciting event that kicks things off to a dramatic climax to the closing resolution.

So, what are your major plot lines?

On the first page, you identified a genre and a central problem. This will be your "A Plot."

If you have a love interest character, and romance is not your A Plot, it will probably be your "B Plot."

Your next most substantial subplot is your "C Plot."

Major Plot Lines		
	Genre	Summary
A Plot		
B Plot		
C Plot		

Basics > Characters > Major > Minor > **Plots** > Timelines > Subplots > Acts > Scenes

Plot Lines

Milestone	**A** Plot
Act 1	
Set up **Normal World**	
Opportunity incites	
P to make a decision	
P's **Predicament** builds	
to **Engaging Incident**, and	
P commits to story goal	
Act 2	
Set up **Adventure World**	
and how **P** fits in	
P's 1st plan (and hurdles)	
Mid-Point Reveal	
(**A** (or **P**) is _____ !)	

P = Protagonist   **A** = Antagonist

Basics > Characters > Major > Minor > **Plots** > Timelines > Subplots > Acts > Scenes

Plot Lines

B Plot	**C** Plot

Basics > Characters > Major > Minor > **Plots** > Timelines > Subplots > Acts > Scenes

Plot Outlines

Milestone	**A** Plot
Act 2.2	
Plan 2 – **Impossible Tasks**	
Ends in **Crisis**	
P gives up/doubts the goal	
Act 3	
Reveal/Assist to **P**	
P is made new, recommits	
Last push leads to	
Climax battle	
(only new **P** could win)	
Resolution and **Aftermath**	

P = Protagonist   **A** = Antagonist

Basics > Characters > Major > Minor > **Plots** > Timelines > Subplots > Acts > Scenes

Plot Outlines

B Plot	**C** Plot

Basics > Characters > Major > Minor > **Plots** > **Timelines** > Subplots > Acts > Scenes

Story History

Date	Event	Age of Protagonist

Basics > Characters > Major > Minor > **Plots** > **Timelines** > Subplots > Acts > Scenes

Story Calendar

Day #	Date	Who	Does What?

Basics > Characters > Major > Minor > **Plots** > Timelines > **Subplots** > Acts > Scenes

Setting – Mind Map

How might **Setting** (or physical representations of it) impact your major plot lines and characters?

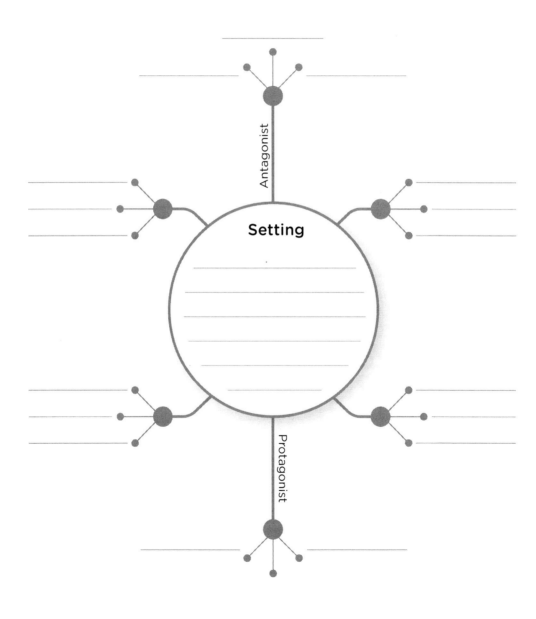

Basics > Characters > Major > Minor > **Plots** > Timelines > **Subplots** > Acts > Scenes

Theme – Mind Map

How might your theme be mirrored in various character arcs and plotlines, in addition to the **Protagonist**'s in order to create meaningful subplots?	What physical objects might symbolize your theme?
	○
	○
	○

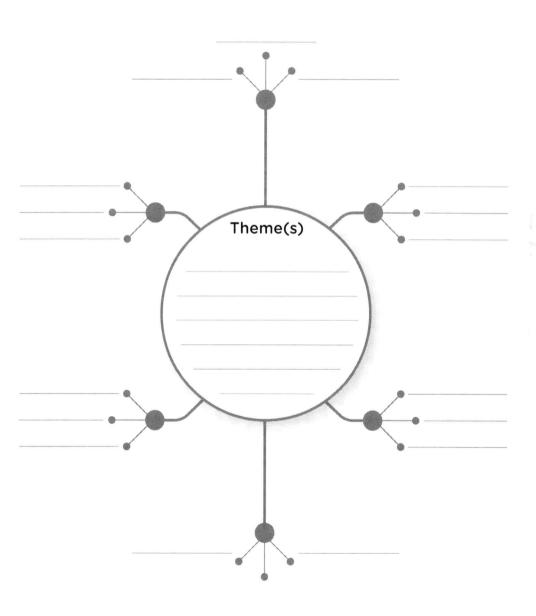

Basics > Characters > Major > Minor > **Plots** > Timelines > **Subplots** > Acts > Scenes

Plot Thread - Mind Map

What other threads (objects, obstacles, feelings, etc.) will be mirrored or repeated across plotlines?

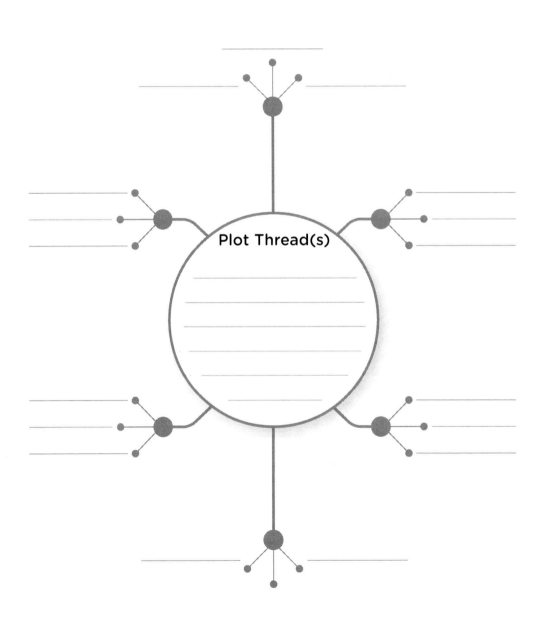

Basics > Characters > Major > Minor > Plots > Timelines > Subplots > **Acts** > Scenes

Act 1 – Key Scenes

Opening Scene – Does it show ⓟ doing something exciting/intriguing, but in character? What questions will it raise for the reader? (Option: Flip to the next section and fill out a Scene Sheet for your opening scene.)

Inciting Incident – Why is it unexpected? Will ⓟ see it as an opportunity? An inconvenience? What decision will ⓟ make in response?	Genre options: ◯ ⓟ gets a message, signal, invite ◯ ⓟ meets someone ◯ ⓟ has a gain (job, inheritance) or loss ◯ ⓐ commits a crime
Engaging Incident – Why is it unexpected? How does it cut off ⓟ's options? What decision does ⓟ make in response?	Genre options: ◯ ⓟ gets obligation ◯ ⓟ gets exiled (or trapped) ◯ ⓟ flees (or pursues ⓐ) ◯ Lovers forced to work together ◯ ⓟ gets the case, mystery

ⓟ = Protagonist   ⓐ = Antagonist

Basics > Characters > Major > Minor > Plots > Timelines > Subplots > **Acts** > Scenes

Act 1 – Overview

Normal World:	Scene Ideas
	○
	○
	○
Audience will relate to ⓟ because:	○
	○
	○
	○
Genre Requirements for Act 1 (meet, murder, discover, flee):	○
	○
	○
	○
Inciting Incident:	○
	○
	○
	○
Engaging Incident:	○
	○
	○
	○
ⓟ's Story Goal:	○
	○
	○
	○
What will hint at the direction of ⓟ's character change?	○
	○
	○
	○

ⓟ = Protagonist   ⓐ = Antagonist

Basics > Characters > Major > Minor > Plots > Timelines > Subplots > **Acts** > Scenes

Act 2.1 – Overview

Adventure World:	Scene Ideas:
	○
	○
	○
How is ⓟ a "fish out of water?"	○
	○
	○
	○
Genre Requirements for the first half of Act 2 (kiss/sex, murder, red herring):	○
	○
	○
	○
What plan does ⓟ make to achieve the story goal?	○
	○
	○
	○
What obstacles will the plan face?	○
	○
	○
	○
Will ⓟ's plan enjoy a moment of success?	○
	○
	○
	○
What game-changer will ⓟ learn at the **Mid-Point**?	○
	○
	○
	○
How are ⓟ's values/fears/(mis)belief affected?	○
	○
	○
	○

ⓟ = Protagonist   ⓐ = Antagonist

Basics > Characters > Major > Minor > Plots > Timelines > Subplots > **Acts** > Scenes

Act 2.2 – Overview

	Scene Ideas:
What new plan does ⓟ make in response to **Mid-Point**?	○ ○ ○
What new plan does ⓐ make?	○ ○ ○ ○
Genre Requirements for the second half of Act 2 (lovers split, praise for villain, death of ally and/or near death of ⓟ):	○ ○ ○ ○
Will you have **Subplots** carry Act 2.2? How will they advance the A Plot?	○ ○ ○ ○
Will ⓟ's new plan succeed or fail? What scene will show this?	○ ○ ○ ○
If ⓟ's new plan fails, why does it end in **Crisis**?	○ ○ ○ ○
If ⓟ's plan succeeds, what **New Twist** will drive Act 3?	○ ○ ○ ○
Why might ⓟ (temporarily) falter or give up the story goal?	○ ○ ○ ○

ⓟ = Protagonist   ⓐ = Antagonist

Basics > Characters > Major > Minor > Plots > Timelines > Subplots > **Acts** > Scenes

Act 3 – Key Scenes

Climax — Win, lose or draw?

◯ **P** defeats **A**   ◯ **P** defeats **A** but sacrifices character change or an important subgoal to do so

◯ **A** defeats **P**   ◯ **A** defeats **P**, but **P** achieves character change or an important subgoal

How might the **Inciting Incident** foreshadow the **Climax** scene?

Resolution

P   WINS / LOSES   the main story goal.

P is rewarded with: ◯ wealth   ◯ immortality   ◯ love   ◯ enlightenment   ◯ _____

P is punished with: ◯ death   ◯ enslavement   ◯ injury   ◯ loss   ◯ _____

How might the **Engaging Incident** foreshadow the **Resolution?**

Final Scene – How will it compare/contrast with **Opening Scene**?

P = Protagonist   **A** = Antagonist

Basics > Characters > Major > Minor > Plots > Timelines > Subplots > **Acts** > Scenes

Act 3 - Overview

What will **P** learn that gives hope of success?	Scene Ideas: ○ ○ ○
Genre Requirements for Act 3 (ticking clock, proof of love, epic battle):	○ ○ ○ ○
What weapon/supplies/info must **P** acquire?	○ ○ ○ ○
Where will the final conflict take place?	○ ○ ○ ○
Will **P** win?	○ ○ ○ ○
P's self-revelation? **A**? Other?	○ ○ ○ ○
What scene will show **P** achieving the story goal?	○ ○ ○ ○
What scene will show **P** acting in (new) character?	○ ○ ○ ○

P = Protagonist   **A** = Antagonist

Scene: _____ #____ ❏ **A** Plot   ❏ **B** Plot   ❏ **C** Plot

Participants / Scene Goals:

○
○
○
○

Time & Place:

Scene Summary: (Action, Reaction, ...)

How will scene upset/surprise?

How will scene impact 🅿?

Unexpected Reaction:

Emotional Charge of Scene (for 🅿):

+ / **−**

Therefore:

🅿 = Protagonist   🅐 = Antagonist

Scene Notes

Scene: _____ #____ ☐ **A** Plot   ☐ **B** Plot   ☐ **C** Plot

Participants / Scene Goals:

○ _____
○ _____
○ _____
○ _____

Time & Place:

How will scene upset/surprise?

How will scene impact **P**?

Emotional Charge of Scene (for **P**):

+ / **−**

Scene Summary: (Action, Reaction, ...)

Unexpected Reaction:

Therefore:

P = Protagonist   **A** = Antagonist

Scene Notes

Scene: _____ #____ ☐ **A** Plot ☐ **B** Plot ☐ **C** Plot

Participants / Scene Goals:

○ _____
○ _____
○ _____
○ _____

Time & Place:	Scene Summary: (Action, Reaction, ...)
How will scene upset/surprise?	
How will scene impact ⓟ?	
	Unexpected Reaction:
Emotional Charge of Scene (for ⓟ): **+** / **−**	Therefore:

ⓟ = Protagonist   ⓐ = Antagonist

Scene Notes

Scene: _____ #____ ❏ **A** Plot   ❏ **B** Plot   ❏ **C** Plot

Participants / Scene Goals:

○ _____

○ _____

○ _____

○ _____

Time & Place:

How will scene upset/surprise?

How will scene impact ⓟ?

Scene Summary: (Action, Reaction, ...)

Unexpected Reaction:

Emotional Charge of Scene (for ⓟ):

+ / **−**

Therefore:

ⓟ = Protagonist   ⓐ = Antagonist

Scene Notes

Scene: _____ #____ ❏ **A** Plot ❏ **B** Plot ❏ **C** Plot

Participants / Scene Goals:

○
○
○
○

Time & Place:	Scene Summary: (Action, Reaction, ...)
How will scene upset/surprise?	
How will scene impact ⓟ?	
	Unexpected Reaction:
Emotional Charge of Scene (for ⓟ): ✚ / ▬	Therefore:

ⓟ = Protagonist   ⓐ = Antagonist

Scene Notes

Scene: _____ #____ ☐ **A** Plot ☐ **B** Plot ☐ **C** Plot

Participants / Scene Goals:

○ _____

○ _____

○ _____

○ _____

Time & Place:	Scene Summary: (Action, Reaction, ...)
How will scene upset/surprise?	
How will scene impact ⓟ?	
	Unexpected Reaction:
Emotional Charge of Scene (for ⓟ): **+** / **−**	Therefore:

ⓟ = Protagonist   ⓐ = Antagonist

Scene Notes

Scene: _____ #____ ❏ **A** Plot   ❏ **B** Plot   ❏ **C** Plot

Participants / Scene Goals:

◯ _____

◯ _____

◯ _____

◯ _____

Time & Place:	Scene Summary: (Action, Reaction, ...)
How will scene upset/surprise?	
How will scene impact Ⓟ?	
	Unexpected Reaction:
Emotional Charge of Scene (for Ⓟ): **+** / **−**	Therefore:

Ⓟ = Protagonist   Ⓐ = Antagonist

Scene Notes

Scene: _____ #____ ❏ **A** Plot ❏ **B** Plot ❏ **C** Plot

Participants / Scene Goals:

◯
◯
◯
◯

Time & Place:	Scene Summary: (Action, Reaction, ...)
How will scene upset/surprise?	
How will scene impact 🅟?	
	Unexpected Reaction:
Emotional Charge of Scene (for 🅟): **+** / **−**	Therefore:

🅟 = Protagonist   🅐 = Antagonist

Scene Notes

Scene: _____ #____ ☐ **A** Plot ☐ **B** Plot ☐ **C** Plot

Participants / Scene Goals:

○ _____

○ _____

○ _____

○ _____

Time & Place:	Scene Summary: (Action, Reaction, ...)
How will scene upset/surprise?	
How will scene impact ⓟ?	
	Unexpected Reaction:
Emotional Charge of Scene (for ⓟ): **+** / **−**	Therefore:

ⓟ = Protagonist   ⓐ = Antagonist

Scene Notes

Scene: _____ #____ ☐ **A** Plot ☐ **B** Plot ☐ **C** Plot

Participants / Scene Goals:

○ _____
○ _____
○ _____
○ _____

Time & Place:	Scene Summary: (Action, Reaction, ...)
How will scene upset/surprise?	
How will scene impact 🅿 ?	
	Unexpected Reaction:
Emotional Charge of Scene (for 🅿): ➕ / ➖	Therefore:

🅿 = Protagonist   🅐 = Antagonist

Scene Notes

Scene: _____ #____ ❏ **A** Plot ❏ **B** Plot ❏ **C** Plot

Participants / Scene Goals:

○ _____

○ _____

○ _____

○ _____

Time & Place:

Scene Summary: (Action, Reaction, …)

How will scene upset/surprise?

How will scene impact **P**?

Unexpected Reaction:

Emotional Charge of Scene (for **P**):

+ / **−**

Therefore:

P = Protagonist   **A** = Antagonist

Scene Notes

Scene: _____ #____ ☐ **A** Plot ☐ **B** Plot ☐ **C** Plot

Participants / Scene Goals:

○ _____
○ _____
○ _____
○ _____

Time & Place:

How will scene upset/surprise?

How will scene impact ⓟ?

Scene Summary: (Action, Reaction, ...)

Unexpected Reaction:

Emotional Charge of Scene (for ⓟ):

+ / **−**

Therefore:

ⓟ = Protagonist   ⓐ = Antagonist

Scene Notes

Scene: _____ #____ ☐ **A** Plot ☐ **B** Plot ☐ **C** Plot

Participants / Scene Goals:

○

○

○

○

Time & Place:

How will scene upset/surprise?

How will scene impact 🅿?

Emotional Charge of Scene (for 🅿):

+ / **−**

Scene Summary: (Action, Reaction, ...)

Unexpected Reaction:

Therefore:

🅿 = Protagonist   🄰 = Antagonist

Scene Notes

Scene:_____ #____ ☐ **A** Plot ☐ **B** Plot ☐ **C** Plot

Participants / Scene Goals:

○ _____

○ _____

○ _____

○ _____

Time & Place:	Scene Summary: (Action, Reaction, ...)
How will scene upset/surprise?	
How will scene impact ⓟ?	
	Unexpected Reaction:
Emotional Charge of Scene (for ⓟ): **+** / **−**	Therefore:

ⓟ = Protagonist ⓐ = Antagonist

Scene Notes

Scene: _____ #____ ☐ **A** Plot ☐ **B** Plot ☐ **C** Plot

Participants / Scene Goals:

○ _____

○ _____

○ _____

○ _____

Time & Place:

Scene Summary: (Action, Reaction, ...)

How will scene upset/surprise?

How will scene impact ⓟ?

Unexpected Reaction:

Emotional Charge of Scene (for ⓟ):

+ / **−**

Therefore:

ⓟ = Protagonist   ⓐ = Antagonist

Scene Notes

Scene: _____ #____ ❐ **A** Plot   ❐ **B** Plot   ❐ **C** Plot

Participants / Scene Goals:

○ _____

○ _____

○ _____

○ _____

Time & Place:

How will scene upset/surprise?

How will scene impact 🅿?

Scene Summary: (Action, Reaction, ...)

Unexpected Reaction:

Emotional Charge of Scene (for 🅿):

+ / **−**

Therefore:

🅿 = Protagonist   🅐 = Antagonist

Scene Notes

Scene: _____ #____ ☐ **A** Plot ☐ **B** Plot ☐ **C** Plot

Participants / Scene Goals:

○ _____
○ _____
○ _____
○ _____

Time & Place:

How will scene upset/surprise?

How will scene impact ⓟ?

Emotional Charge of Scene (for ⓟ):

+ / **−**

Scene Summary: (Action, Reaction, ...)

Unexpected Reaction:

Therefore:

ⓟ = Protagonist   ⓐ = Antagonist

Scene Notes

Scene: _____ #____ ☐ **A** Plot ☐ **B** Plot ☐ **C** Plot

Participants / Scene Goals:

○
○
○
○

Time & Place:

How will scene upset/surprise?

How will scene impact 🅟?

Scene Summary: (Action, Reaction, ...)

Unexpected Reaction:

Emotional Charge of Scene (for 🅟):

+ / **−**

Therefore:

🅟 = Protagonist 🅐 = Antagonist

Scene Notes

Scene: _____ #____ ☐ **A** Plot ☐ **B** Plot ☐ **C** Plot

Participants / Scene Goals:

○ _____

○ _____

○ _____

○ _____

Time & Place:

How will scene upset/surprise?

How will scene impact 🅟?

Emotional Charge of Scene (for 🅟):

+ / **−**

Scene Summary: (Action, Reaction, ...)

Unexpected Reaction:

Therefore:

🅟 = Protagonist   🅐 = Antagonist

Scene Notes

Scene:_____ #____ ☐ **A** Plot ☐ **B** Plot ☐ **C** Plot

Participants / Scene Goals:

○

○

○

○

Time & Place:

Scene Summary: (Action, Reaction, ...)

How will scene upset/surprise?

How will scene impact 🅿?

Unexpected Reaction:

Emotional Charge of Scene (for 🅿):

Therefore:

+ / **−**

🅿 = Protagonist   🅐 = Antagonist

Scene Notes

Scene: _____ #____ ❒ **A** Plot ❒ **B** Plot ❒ **C** Plot

Participants / Scene Goals:

○ _____

○ _____

○ _____

○ _____

Time & Place:	Scene Summary: (Action, Reaction, ...)
How will scene upset/surprise?	
How will scene impact 🅟?	
	Unexpected Reaction:
Emotional Charge of Scene (for 🅟): **+** / **−**	Therefore:

🅟 = Protagonist   🅐 = Antagonist

Scene Notes

Scene: _____ #____ ❏ **A** Plot ❏ **B** Plot ❏ **C** Plot

Participants / Scene Goals:

◯ _____

◯ _____

◯ _____

◯ _____

Time & Place:	Scene Summary: (Action, Reaction, ...)
How will scene upset/surprise?	
How will scene impact ⓟ?	
	Unexpected Reaction:
Emotional Charge of Scene (for ⓟ): **+** / **−**	Therefore:

ⓟ = Protagonist   ⓐ = Antagonist

Scene Notes

Scene: _____ #____ ❏ **A** Plot ❏ **B** Plot ❏ **C** Plot

Participants / Scene Goals:

○
○
○
○

Time & Place:

How will scene upset/surprise?

How will scene impact 🅿?

Scene Summary: (Action, Reaction, ...)

Unexpected Reaction:

Emotional Charge of Scene (for 🅿):

+ / **−**

Therefore:

🅿 = Protagonist   🅐 = Antagonist

Scene Notes

Scene: _____ #____ ❏ **A** Plot ❏ **B** Plot ❏ **C** Plot

Participants / Scene Goals:

○ _____
○ _____
○ _____
○ _____

Time & Place:	Scene Summary: (Action, Reaction, ...)
How will scene upset/surprise?	
How will scene impact ⓟ?	
	Unexpected Reaction:
Emotional Charge of Scene (for ⓟ): **+** / **−**	Therefore:

ⓟ = Protagonist   Ⓐ = Antagonist

Scene Notes

Scene: _____ #____ ☐ **A** Plot ☐ **B** Plot ☐ **C** Plot

Participants / Scene Goals:

○ _____
○ _____
○ _____
○ _____

Time & Place:

Scene Summary: (Action, Reaction, ...)

How will scene upset/surprise?

How will scene impact ⓟ?

Unexpected Reaction:

Emotional Charge of Scene (for ⓟ):

+ / **−**

Therefore:

ⓟ = Protagonist   ⓐ = Antagonist

Scene Notes

Scene: _____ #____ ❏ **A** Plot   ❏ **B** Plot   ❏ **C** Plot

Participants / Scene Goals:

○ _____

○ _____

○ _____

○ _____

Time & Place:	Scene Summary: (Action, Reaction, ...)
How will scene upset/surprise?	
How will scene impact ⓟ?	
	Unexpected Reaction:
Emotional Charge of Scene (for ⓟ): ➕ / ➖	Therefore:

ⓟ = Protagonist   ⓐ = Antagonist

Scene Notes

Scene: _____ #____ ☐ **A** Plot   ☐ **B** Plot   ☐ **C** Plot

Participants / Scene Goals:

○ _____
○ _____
○ _____
○ _____

Time & Place:	Scene Summary: (Action, Reaction, …)
How will scene upset/surprise?	
How will scene impact ⓟ?	
	Unexpected Reaction:
Emotional Charge of Scene (for ⓟ): **+** / **−**	Therefore:

ⓟ = Protagonist   ⓐ = Antagonist

Scene Notes

Scene: _____ #____ ❏ **A** Plot   ❏ **B** Plot   ❏ **C** Plot

Participants / Scene Goals:

○ _____

○ _____

○ _____

○ _____

Time & Place: | Scene Summary: (Action, Reaction, ...)

How will scene upset/surprise?

How will scene impact ⓟ?

| Unexpected Reaction:

Emotional Charge of Scene (for ⓟ): | Therefore:

+ / **−**

ⓟ = Protagonist   ⓐ = Antagonist

Scene Notes

Scene: _____ #____ ❏ **A** Plot ❏ **B** Plot ❏ **C** Plot

Participants / Scene Goals:

- ○
- ○
- ○
- ○

Time & Place:

How will scene upset/surprise?

How will scene impact **P**?

Scene Summary: (Action, Reaction, ...)

Unexpected Reaction:

Emotional Charge of Scene (for **P**):

+ / **−**

Therefore:

P = Protagonist   **A** = Antagonist

Scene Notes

Scene: _____ #____ ❏ **A** Plot ❏ **B** Plot ❏ **C** Plot

Participants / Scene Goals:

◯ _____

◯ _____

◯ _____

◯ _____

| Time & Place: | Scene Summary: (Action, Reaction, …) |

How will scene upset/surprise?

How will scene impact ⓟ?

Unexpected Reaction:

Emotional Charge of Scene (for ⓟ):

+ / **−**

Therefore:

ⓟ = Protagonist ⓐ = Antagonist

Scene Notes

Scene: _____ #____ ☐ **A** Plot ☐ **B** Plot ☐ **C** Plot

Participants / Scene Goals:

○ _____

○ _____

○ _____

○ _____

Time & Place:

Scene Summary: (Action, Reaction, ...)

How will scene upset/surprise?

How will scene impact ⓟ?

Unexpected Reaction:

Emotional Charge of Scene (for ⓟ):

+ / **−**

Therefore:

ⓟ = Protagonist   ⓐ = Antagonist

Scene Notes

Scene: _____ #____ ❏ **A** Plot ❏ **B** Plot ❏ **C** Plot

Participants / Scene Goals:

◯ _____

◯ _____

◯ _____

◯ _____

Time & Place:	Scene Summary: (Action, Reaction, ...)
How will scene upset/surprise?	
How will scene impact 🅟?	
	Unexpected Reaction:
Emotional Charge of Scene (for 🅟): **+** / **−**	Therefore:

🅟 = Protagonist 🅐 = Antagonist

Scene Notes

Scene: _____ #____ ❑ **A** Plot   ❑ **B** Plot   ❑ **C** Plot

Participants / Scene Goals:

○ _____

○ _____

○ _____

○ _____

Time & Place:

Scene Summary: (Action, Reaction, ...)

How will scene upset/surprise?

How will scene impact ⓟ?

Unexpected Reaction:

Emotional Charge of Scene (for ⓟ):

+ / **−**

Therefore:

ⓟ = Protagonist   ⓐ = Antagonist

Scene Notes

Scene: _____ #____ ☐ **A** Plot   ☐ **B** Plot   ☐ **C** Plot

Participants / Scene Goals:

○ _____
○ _____
○ _____
○ _____

Time & Place:	Scene Summary: (Action, Reaction, …)
How will scene upset/surprise?	
How will scene impact Ⓟ?	
	Unexpected Reaction:
Emotional Charge of Scene (for Ⓟ): **+** / **−**	Therefore:

Ⓟ = Protagonist   Ⓐ = Antagonist

Scene Notes

Scene: _____ #____ ☐ **A** Plot   ☐ **B** Plot   ☐ **C** Plot

Participants / Scene Goals:

○ _____
○ _____
○ _____
○ _____

Time & Place:

How will scene upset/surprise?

How will scene impact 🅟?

Emotional Charge of Scene (for 🅟):

+ / **−**

Scene Summary: (Action, Reaction, ...)

Unexpected Reaction:

Therefore:

🅟 = Protagonist   🅐 = Antagonist

Scene Notes

Scene: _____ #____ ☐ **A** Plot   ☐ **B** Plot   ☐ **C** Plot

Participants / Scene Goals:

○ _____
○ _____
○ _____
○ _____

Time & Place:

Scene Summary: (Action, Reaction, ...)

How will scene upset/surprise?

How will scene impact 🅟?

Unexpected Reaction:

Emotional Charge of Scene (for 🅟):

+ / **−**

Therefore:

🅟 = Protagonist   🅐 = Antagonist

Scene Notes

Scene: _____ #____ ❒ **A** Plot   ❒ **B** Plot   ❒ **C** Plot

Participants / Scene Goals:

○ _____

○ _____

○ _____

○ _____

Time & Place:	Scene Summary: (Action, Reaction, …)
How will scene upset/surprise?	
How will scene impact ⓟ?	
	Unexpected Reaction:
Emotional Charge of Scene (for ⓟ): ➕ / ➖	Therefore:

ⓟ = Protagonist   ⓐ = Antagonist

Scene Notes

Scene: _____ #____ ❏ **A** Plot ❏ **B** Plot ❏ **C** Plot

Participants / Scene Goals:

○ _____

○ _____

○ _____

○ _____

Time & Place:

Scene Summary: (Action, Reaction, ...)

How will scene upset/surprise?

How will scene impact Ⓟ?

Unexpected Reaction:

Emotional Charge of Scene (for Ⓟ):

+ / **−**

Therefore:

Ⓟ = Protagonist   Ⓐ = Antagonist

Scene Notes

Scene: _____ #____ ❏ **A** Plot ❏ **B** Plot ❏ **C** Plot

Participants / Scene Goals:

○
○
○
○

Time & Place:

How will scene upset/surprise?

How will scene impact ⓟ?

Scene Summary: (Action, Reaction, ...)

Unexpected Reaction:

Emotional Charge of Scene (for ⓟ):

+ / **−**

Therefore:

ⓟ = Protagonist   ⓐ = Antagonist

Scene Notes

Scene: _____ #____ ❐ **A** Plot ❐ **B** Plot ❐ **C** Plot

Participants / Scene Goals:

◯
◯
◯
◯

Time & Place:

Scene Summary: (Action, Reaction, …)

How will scene upset/surprise?

How will scene impact ⓟ?

Unexpected Reaction:

Emotional Charge of Scene (for ⓟ):

➕ / ➖

Therefore:

ⓟ = Protagonist   ⓐ = Antagonist

Scene Notes

Scene: _____ #____ ❑ **A** Plot ❑ **B** Plot ❑ **C** Plot

Participants / Scene Goals:

◯
◯
◯
◯

Time & Place:

How will scene upset/surprise?

How will scene impact ⓟ?

Scene Summary: (Action, Reaction, …)

Unexpected Reaction:

Emotional Charge of Scene (for ⓟ):

➕ / ➖

Therefore:

ⓟ = Protagonist   ⓐ = Antagonist

Scene Notes

Scene: _____ #____ ☐ **A** Plot ☐ **B** Plot ☐ **C** Plot

Participants / Scene Goals:

○ _____

○ _____

○ _____

○ _____

Time & Place:

How will scene upset/surprise?

How will scene impact ⓟ?

Emotional Charge of Scene (for ⓟ):

+ / **−**

Scene Summary: (Action, Reaction, ...)

Unexpected Reaction:

Therefore:

ⓟ = Protagonist   ⓐ = Antagonist

Scene Notes

Scene: _____ #____ ☐ **A** Plot   ☐ **B** Plot   ☐ **C** Plot

Participants / Scene Goals:

○ _____

○ _____

○ _____

○ _____

Time & Place:

Scene Summary: (Action, Reaction, ...)

How will scene upset/surprise?

How will scene impact **P**?

Unexpected Reaction:

Emotional Charge of Scene (for **P**):

+ / **−**

Therefore:

P = Protagonist   **A** = Antagonist

Scene Notes

Scene: _____ #____ ☐ **A** Plot   ☐ **B** Plot   ☐ **C** Plot

Participants / Scene Goals:

- ○
- ○
- ○
- ○

Time & Place:	Scene Summary: (Action, Reaction, ...)
How will scene upset/surprise?	
How will scene impact ⓟ?	
	Unexpected Reaction:
Emotional Charge of Scene (for ⓟ): **+** / **−**	Therefore:

ⓟ = Protagonist   ⓐ = Antagonist

Scene Notes

Scene: _____ #____ ☐ **A** Plot   ☐ **B** Plot   ☐ **C** Plot

Participants / Scene Goals:

○ _____

○ _____

○ _____

○ _____

Time & Place:	Scene Summary: (Action, Reaction, …)
How will scene upset/surprise?	
How will scene impact ⓟ?	
	Unexpected Reaction:
Emotional Charge of Scene (for ⓟ): **+** / **−**	Therefore:

ⓟ = Protagonist   ⓐ = Antagonist

Scene Notes

Scene: _____ #____ ☐ **A** Plot ☐ **B** Plot ☐ **C** Plot

Participants / Scene Goals:

○ _____

○ _____

○ _____

○ _____

Time & Place:	Scene Summary: (Action, Reaction, …)
How will scene upset/surprise?	
How will scene impact ⓟ?	
	Unexpected Reaction:
Emotional Charge of Scene (for ⓟ): **+** / **−**	Therefore:

ⓟ = Protagonist   ⓐ = Antagonist

Scene Notes

Scene: _____ #____ ☐ **A** Plot   ☐ **B** Plot   ☐ **C** Plot

Participants / Scene Goals:

○ _____

○ _____

○ _____

○ _____

Time & Place:	Scene Summary: (Action, Reaction, ...)
How will scene upset/surprise?	
How will scene impact 🅿?	
	Unexpected Reaction:
Emotional Charge of Scene (for 🅿): **+** / **−**	Therefore:

🅿 = Protagonist   🅐 = Antagonist

Scene Notes

Scene: _____ #____   ☐ **A** Plot   ☐ **B** Plot   ☐ **C** Plot

Participants / Scene Goals:

○ _____
○ _____
○ _____
○ _____

Time & Place:	Scene Summary: (Action, Reaction, ...)
How will scene upset/surprise?	
How will scene impact ⓟ?	
	Unexpected Reaction:
Emotional Charge of Scene (for ⓟ): **+** / **−**	Therefore:

ⓟ = Protagonist   ⓐ = Antagonist

Scene Notes

Scene: _____ #____ ☐ **A** Plot   ☐ **B** Plot   ☐ **C** Plot

Participants / Scene Goals:

○ _____

○ _____

○ _____

○ _____

| Time & Place: | Scene Summary: (Action, Reaction, ...) |

How will scene upset/surprise?

How will scene impact ⓟ?

Unexpected Reaction:

Emotional Charge of Scene (for ⓟ):

+ / **−**

Therefore:

ⓟ = Protagonist   ⓐ = Antagonist

Scene Notes

Scene:_____ #____ ☐ **A** Plot   ☐ **B** Plot   ☐ **C** Plot

Participants / Scene Goals:

○ _____
○ _____
○ _____
○ _____

Time & Place:	Scene Summary: (Action, Reaction, ...)
How will scene upset/surprise?	
How will scene impact ⓟ?	
	Unexpected Reaction:
Emotional Charge of Scene (for ⓟ): **+** / **−**	Therefore:

ⓟ = Protagonist   ⓐ = Antagonist

Scene Notes

Scene: _____ #____ ❏ **A** Plot   ❏ **B** Plot   ❏ **C** Plot

Participants / Scene Goals:

○
○
○
○

Time & Place:

How will scene upset/surprise?

How will scene impact ⓟ?

Scene Summary: (Action, Reaction, …)

Unexpected Reaction:

Emotional Charge of Scene (for ⓟ):

+ / **−**

Therefore:

ⓟ = Protagonist   ⓐ = Antagonist

Scene Notes

Scene: _____ #____ ❒ **A** Plot   ❒ **B** Plot   ❒ **C** Plot

Participants / Scene Goals:

○ _____

○ _____

○ _____

○ _____

| Time & Place: | Scene Summary: (Action, Reaction, ...) |

How will scene upset/surprise?

How will scene impact ⓟ?

Unexpected Reaction:

Emotional Charge of Scene (for ⓟ):

+ / **−**

Therefore:

ⓟ = Protagonist   ⓐ = Antagonist

Scene Notes

Scene: _____ #____ ❏ **A** Plot ❏ **B** Plot ❏ **C** Plot

Participants / Scene Goals:

◯ _____
◯ _____
◯ _____
◯ _____

Time & Place:	Scene Summary: (Action, Reaction, …)
How will scene upset/surprise?	
How will scene impact ⓟ?	
	Unexpected Reaction:
Emotional Charge of Scene (for ⓟ): **+** / **−**	Therefore:

ⓟ = Protagonist   ⓐ = Antagonist

Scene Notes

Scene: _____ #____ ❒ **A** Plot   ❒ **B** Plot   ❒ **C** Plot

Participants / Scene Goals:

◯ _____

◯ _____

◯ _____

◯ _____

Time & Place:

Scene Summary: (Action, Reaction, ...)

How will scene upset/surprise?

How will scene impact ⓟ?

Unexpected Reaction:

Emotional Charge of Scene (for ⓟ):

+ / **−**

Therefore:

ⓟ = Protagonist   ⓐ = Antagonist

Scene Notes

Scene: _____ #____ ☐ **A** Plot   ☐ **B** Plot   ☐ **C** Plot

Participants / Scene Goals:

○ _____
○ _____
○ _____
○ _____

Time & Place:	Scene Summary: (Action, Reaction, ...)
How will scene upset/surprise?	
How will scene impact ⓟ?	
	Unexpected Reaction:
Emotional Charge of Scene (for ⓟ): **+** / **−**	Therefore:

ⓟ = Protagonist   ⓐ = Antagonist

Scene Notes

Scene: _____ #____ ☐ **A** Plot   ☐ **B** Plot   ☐ **C** Plot

Participants / Scene Goals:

◯ _____
◯ _____
◯ _____
◯ _____

| Time & Place: | Scene Summary: (Action, Reaction, ...) |

How will scene upset/surprise?

How will scene impact ⓟ?

Unexpected Reaction:

Emotional Charge of Scene (for ⓟ):

+ / **−**

Therefore:

ⓟ = Protagonist   ⓐ = Antagonist

Scene Notes

Scene: _____ #____ ☐ **A** Plot   ☐ **B** Plot   ☐ **C** Plot

Participants / Scene Goals:

○ _____

○ _____

○ _____

○ _____

Time & Place:	Scene Summary: (Action, Reaction, ...)
How will scene upset/surprise?	
How will scene impact ⓟ?	
	Unexpected Reaction:
Emotional Charge of Scene (for ⓟ): **+** / **−**	Therefore:

ⓟ = Protagonist   ⓐ = Antagonist

Scene Notes

Scene:_____ #____ ☐ **A** Plot   ☐ **B** Plot   ☐ **C** Plot

Participants / Scene Goals:

○
○
○
○

Time & Place:	Scene Summary: (Action, Reaction, …)
How will scene upset/surprise?	
How will scene impact 🅟?	
	Unexpected Reaction:
Emotional Charge of Scene (for 🅟): **+** / **−**	Therefore:

🅟 = Protagonist   🅐 = Antagonist

Scene Notes

Scene: _____ #____ ☐ **A** Plot   ☐ **B** Plot   ☐ **C** Plot

Participants / Scene Goals:

○ _____
○ _____
○ _____
○ _____

Time & Place:	Scene Summary: (Action, Reaction, ...)
How will scene upset/surprise?	
How will scene impact 🅿?	
	Unexpected Reaction:
Emotional Charge of Scene (for 🅿): **+** / **−**	Therefore:

🅿 = Protagonist   🅐 = Antagonist

Scene Notes

Scene: _____ #____ ☐ **A** Plot ☐ **B** Plot ☐ **C** Plot

Participants / Scene Goals:

○ _____
○ _____
○ _____
○ _____

Time & Place:	Scene Summary: (Action, Reaction, …)
How will scene upset/surprise?	
How will scene impact 🅟?	
	Unexpected Reaction:
Emotional Charge of Scene (for 🅟): **+** / **−**	Therefore:

🅟 = Protagonist   🅐 = Antagonist

Scene Notes

Love your NovelReady planner?

Please help us spread the word on social media and follow us at **www.facebook.com/novelready**.

Got suggestions?

Go to **www.novelready.com/suggestionbox**.
We aim to tailor our planners to our customers' needs, and we'd love to hear from you!